MYTH BUSTERS

ANIMAL ERRORS

KINGFISHER

KINGFISHER

First Published in 2021 by Kingfisher
A division of Macmillan Children's Books
The Smithson, 6 Briset Street,
London, EC1M 5NR
Associated companies throughout the world
www.panmacmillan.com

ISBN: 978-0-7534-4601-0

Material previously published as *Think Again!*
in 2013.

Text copyright © Clive Gifford 2013, 2021
Illustration copyright © Macmillan
Publishers International Ltd 2013, 2021
Designed by Tall Tree Ltd

9 8 7 6 5 4 3 2
2TR/0821/WKT/UG/128MA

A CIP catalogue record of this book is available
from the British Library.

Printed in Poland

MIX
Paper from
responsible sources
FSC® C116313
FSC
www.fsc.org

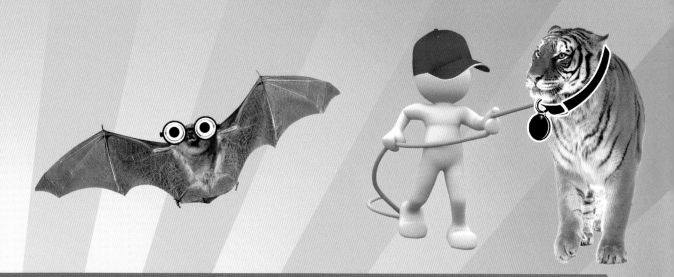

MYTH BUSTERS

ANIMAL ERRORS

CLIVE GIFFORD

CONTENTS

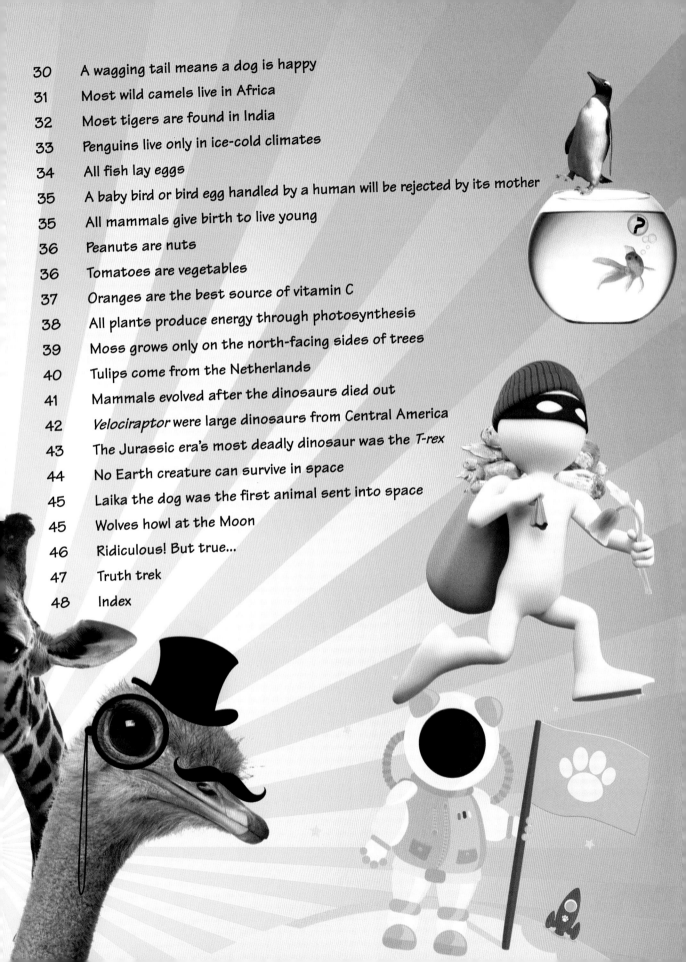

MYTH BUSTERS

INTRODUCTION

Everything you know is wrong*. Some writers get it wrong from the start or they present their opinions as pure fact. Others copy this information without questioning it or shorten and summarize facts from reliable sources, but miss out vital points as a result. A lot of myths and mistakes are spread by word of mouth or via emails, blogs and websites, as many people love gossip and rumours. Over time, the most repeated myths become accepted as facts.

Knowledge is evolving continually. Discoveries about how things work or how things were in the past are being made all the time. The idea of new innovations may seem unlikely or pure science fiction. But amazing developments in technology — such as the Internet, personal communications, space travel and replacement body parts — have quickly become scientific fact.

This book is packed with misconceptions, errors, falsehoods and bonkers theories that have somehow gained status as facts. It explains what the real facts are and, in some cases, how the wrong facts caught on. So if you think everything you know is 100 per cent correct... THINK AGAIN! The truth is out there — only it is sometimes very different to what you thought it was.

*OKAY, NOT QUITE EVERYTHING, BUT A SURPRISINGLY LARGE AMOUNT.

ANIMAL ERRORS

When British naturalist George Shaw was sent a stuffed, duck-billed platypus from Australia in 1799, he thought someone had sewn a duck's beak onto another creature as a joke. But the duck-billed mammal, which lays eggs and has webbed feet, was no hoax. Neither are the plants that eat insects or the squid that's 14m long with an eye the size of your dinner plate.

The natural world continues to surprise us. New species of plants and animals are discovered all the time, with a staggering 18,000 found in 2016 alone. And that's not all. Every year research reveals amazing revelations about many different species and how they live, forcing naturalists to revise their beliefs.

So, if you've ever been told that the blue whale is the biggest living thing on the planet, that bats are blind or ostriches stick their head in the sand, then you've been had. These animal errors are errors indeed. They are simply... not... true.

BEASTLY BELIEFS

ERROR #1

THE BIGGEST LIVING THING IS THE BLUE WHALE

Capable of growing up to 30m in length, the blue whale is an absolute whopper. It is so large that its heart is the size of a small car. To grow to that size, baby blue whales drink as much as 400 litres of milk from their mothers each day.

The blue whale is the biggest ever mammal and the largest animal on Earth, but there are living things that are much larger.

Hyperion is a redwood tree in California, USA, and at 115.61m in height it is the world's tallest tree. General Sherman is a giant sequoia tree with a circumference of 31m, a height of 83.5m and a weight of 1,488 tonnes. That's some chunky trunkies!

Another contender is actually a fungus. *Armillaria solidipes*, also called the honey fungus, is known for its large, capped mushrooms. But most of the fungus spreads out underground. One specimen, found in the USA's Malheur National Forest, Oregon, extends up to 965 hectares – that's more than 1,500 football pitches!

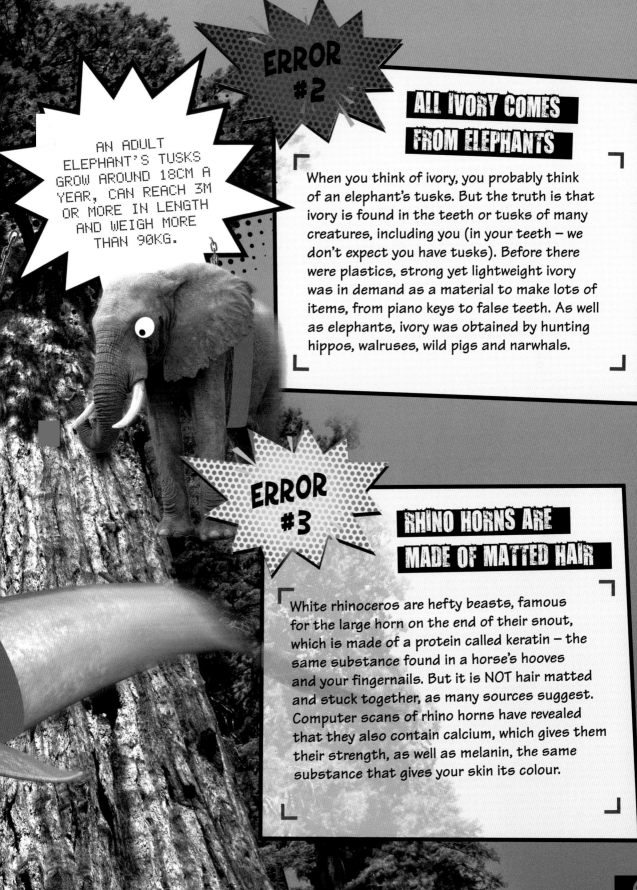

ERROR #2

AN ADULT ELEPHANT'S TUSKS GROW AROUND 18CM A YEAR, CAN REACH 3M OR MORE IN LENGTH AND WEIGH MORE THAN 90KG.

ALL IVORY COMES FROM ELEPHANTS

When you think of ivory, you probably think of an elephant's tusks. But the truth is that ivory is found in the teeth or tusks of many creatures, including you (in your teeth – we don't expect you have tusks). Before there were plastics, strong yet lightweight ivory was in demand as a material to make lots of items, from piano keys to false teeth. As well as elephants, ivory was obtained by hunting hippos, walruses, wild pigs and narwhals.

ERROR #3

RHINO HORNS ARE MADE OF MATTED HAIR

White rhinoceros are hefty beasts, famous for the large horn on the end of their snout, which is made of a protein called keratin – the same substance found in a horse's hooves and your fingernails. But it is NOT hair matted and stuck together, as many sources suggest. Computer scans of rhino horns have revealed that they also contain calcium, which gives them their strength, as well as melanin, the same substance that gives your skin its colour.

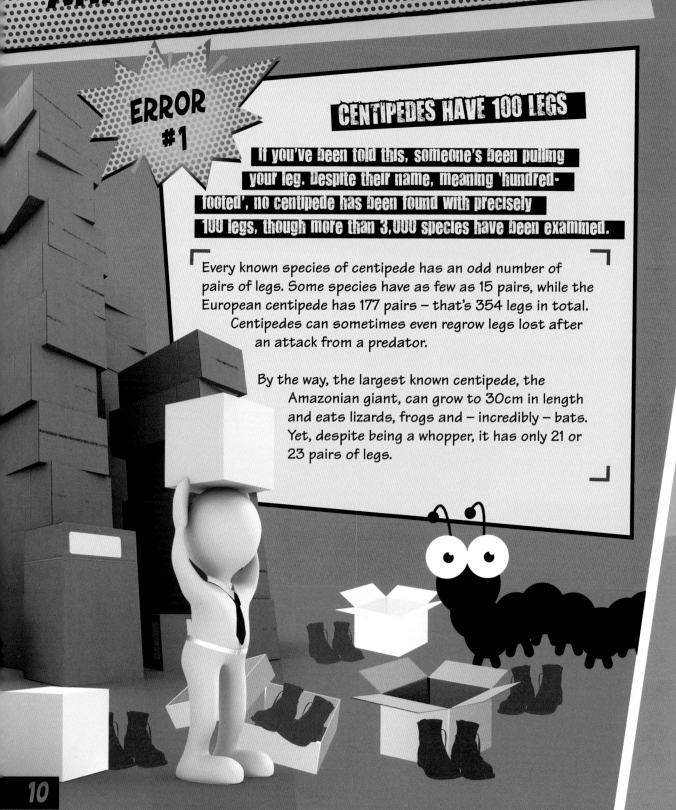

ERROR #1

CENTIPEDES HAVE 100 LEGS

If you've been told this, someone's been pulling your leg. Despite their name, meaning 'hundred-footed', no centipede has been found with precisely 100 legs, though more than 3,000 species have been examined.

Every known species of centipede has an odd number of pairs of legs. Some species have as few as 15 pairs, while the European centipede has 177 pairs – that's 354 legs in total. Centipedes can sometimes even regrow legs lost after an attack from a predator.

By the way, the largest known centipede, the Amazonian giant, can grow to 30cm in length and eats lizards, frogs and – incredibly – bats. Yet, despite being a whopper, it has only 21 or 23 pairs of legs.

CAMELS STORE WATER IN THEIR HUMPS

Don't get the hump, but this is false. Camels are built to survive many days without water and up to three weeks without food. The secret is in the hump (or humps) on their back. Each big lump doesn't hold water – it's a huge store of up to 35kg of fat, and a camel's body converts this fat into energy.

So, how can camels go without water for so long? Camels have many adaptations for life in hot, dry desert areas. Their red blood cells are oval-shaped rather than round, allowing them to flow even when a camel is dehydrated. Also, their kidneys and intestines are very efficient, recovering almost every drop of water from their digestive system. Their nostrils even trap and recycle water vapour in their breath as they breathe out.

A THIRSTY CAMEL CAN GULP DOWN MORE THAN 100 LITRES OF WATER IN LESS THAN 13 MINUTES.

ERROR #3

OSTRICHES STICK THEIR HEADS IN SAND

The old myth goes that, when in danger, ostriches stick their heads in the sand rather than run away. But this would be odd behaviour for a tall creature with sharp vision and long legs. If danger looms, ostriches can sprint at speeds of up to 70km/h.

So where does the myth come from? In the African plains where ostriches live, the landscape is mostly scrubland, not sand. Sometimes ostriches bend down to turn their eggs or swallow pebbles, which help them to digest food. With heat hazes causing the ground to shimmer, it may look like an ostrich's head is disappearing below ground.

THE ELEPHANT BIRDS OF MADAGASCAR WERE THE LARGEST BIRDS - EVER! NOW EXTINCT, THEY WERE 3M TALL AND WEIGHED UP TO 860KG!

FALSE MOVES

ERROR #1

BEARS CANNOT RUN DOWNHILL

Grrrr. This myth makes some naturalists as angry as a grizzly with a thorn in its paw.

Yes, okay... bears' front paws are shorter and less powerful than their back paws – BUT, if they run down a slope, bears don't fall over. Bears are surprisingly fast and nimble for their size, even on hills. Most bears can run at more than 40km/h, about the same as a 100m sprint world record holder, so you're unlikely to outpace them.

DURING HIBERNATION, SOME SPECIES OF BEARS CAN GO FOR 100 DAYS OR SO WITHOUT FOOD, WATER OR GOING TO THE TOILET!

ERROR #2

ELEPHANTS ARE THE ONLY ANIMALS THAT CANNOT JUMP

Some say elephants are far too heavy to jump. Others say that they have no reason to jump. All agree, though, that an elephant cannot jump. But there's a twist. There are other members of the animal kingdom that cannot jump, including three-toed sloths and molluscs such as clams and earthworms. The legs of rhinoceroses and hippopotamuses can leave the ground momentarily while running, but neither can jump from a standing start.

ERROR #3

CROCODILES RUN FASTER THAN PEOPLE

Much of the belief about crocodiles' speed comes from their sudden lunges. But when it comes to real running, the Australian freshwater crocodile is the speed king. It actually gallops like a horse using its short, powerful legs. The fastest recorded speed is 17km/h. Most other crocs tend to slither more slowly on their bellies. According to the Crocodilian Biology Database, 12–14km/h is their maximum speed and this can only be maintained for short bursts. So most people can outrun a crocodile. But it's a risky business!

COLOURFUL CHARACTERS

ERROR #1

BULLS ARE ENRAGED BY THE COLOUR RED

You've seen it in films and cartoons — a character wearing red being chased by a furious bull. But the bull is not in a rage over the colour red.

Bulls are actually colour-blind. In bullfighting, the bull is angry because it has been teased, prodded and sometimes hurt by lances and sharp sticks dug into its body. The bulls aim for the cape because of its movement, not its red colour. They will charge just as furiously at the inside of the cape, which is often yellow.

CHAMELEONS CHANGE COLOUR TO MATCH THEIR SURROUNDINGS

ERROR #2

There are more than 100 species of chameleon and many of them can change the colour of their appearance in just 20 seconds.

Many chameleons, especially male ones, change colour to do the exact opposite of hiding. They're showing off to potential female mates. Some species become a rainbow of pinks, blues, purples and yellows. Chameleons also change colour due to changes in light and temperature. In bright sunlight, many chameleons will turn lighter in colour. This helps to reflect sunlight. If the weather turns cooler, they may turn darker to absorb more of the Sun's energy and help them stay warm.

ERROR #3

POLAR BEARS ARE WHITE

The skin of a polar bear is actually black. It has a close, insulating layer of fur and then, above that, a layer of what looks to be white hair. These 'guard hairs' make up the polar bear's protective outer layer and they are transparent (see-through). Each hair has a hollow core, which reflects and scatters the light hitting it, making it appear white.

ZEBRAS ARE NOT WHITE WITH BLACK STRIPES. SHAVE A ZEBRA AND YOU'LL SEE THAT THEY HAVE BLACK OR VERY DARK GREY SKIN UNDERNEATH THE WHITE HAIR THAT FORMS THE STRIPES.

SENSELESS!

ERROR #1

GOLDFISH HAVE A THREE-SECOND MEMORY

Imagine only remembering what you were doing for three seconds. You wouldn't get anything done! Fortunately, goldfish don't have much to do, but doesn't such a short memory span smell fishy to you?

In 2008, schoolboy Rory Stokes tried an experiment with his goldfish, placing fish food beside a red brick toy in his fish tank each day for three weeks. He stopped for one week, then placed the brick back in the tank again; the goldfish swam over to it expecting food. This proved it had a 604,800-second memory (60 seconds x 60 minutes x 24 hours x 7 days)! Similarly, goldfish at Israel's Institute of Technology were trained to recognize a sound that marked feeding time, and still remembered it five months later.

ERROR #2

BATS ARE BLIND

You're batty if you believe this one! There are more than 1,100 species of bats, which come in two broad types – mega and micro. Megabats are the bigger bats that eat fruit, nectar and small animals. They're definitely not blind since they possess big eyes and rely on their daylight vision to fly and find food.

Microbats tend to have small eyes, cannot see in colour, and use echolocation to navigate and hunt. They send out high-pitched sounds, which bounce off objects, and then detect the returning sounds to calculate their distance from the object. Even with this super-sense microbats still rely on their eyesight to avoid big objects and see across long distances.

BRACKEN CAVE IN SAN ANTONIO, TEXAS, USA, IS HOME TO MORE THAN 20 MILLION MEXICAN FREE-TAILED BATS – THE WORLD'S LARGEST KNOWN BAT COLONY.

ERROR #3

PENGUINS FALL OVER BACKWARDS WHEN WATCHING PLANES FLY OVER THEM

This is the claim that penguins watch aircraft so carefully that they lose their balance. Sounds comical – but if it were the case, it would be a big deal for some penguins who struggle to stand up after falling over.

However, in the year 2000, researchers from the British Antarctic Survey travelled to the island of South Georgia, near Antarctica. Here, they investigated the reaction of 1,000 king penguins to aircraft flying overhead. Some of the birds did watch the planes, but over five weeks, the researchers didn't see a single penguin fall over backwards.

HAVE YOU HEARD?

SNAKE CHARMERS CHARM SNAKES WITH THEIR MUSIC

Once common in bazaars of the Middle East and Asia, snake charming has a long hisssss-tory and may have begun more than 4,000 years ago.

A man plays a flute and sways, luring a large, deadly snake out of a basket. The cobra starts to sway, appearing to keep rhythm with the music. It looks amazing, but is something slippery afoot?

Many people think that charming cannot work because snakes are deaf. Although they don't have external ears like yours, they do have inner ear mechanisms and can sense low-frequency vibrations. However, they are deaf to higher-pitched sounds from musical instruments. It is actually the moving of the charmer that makes the snake sway.

A GIRAFFE'S TONGUE IS ABOUT 50CM LONG, ENABLING IT TO GRASP HIGH BRANCHES AND GULP DOWN LEAVES. AN ADULT GIRAFFE CAN EAT MORE THAN 30KG OF FOLIAGE A DAY. SLURP!

GIRAFFES CANNOT MAKE A SOUND

The tallest land creatures, giraffes, can stand 5–6m in height. They have a 2-metre-long neck, but no vocal cords.

However, they can still make noises. Young giraffe calves can snort and moo, while adult giraffes occasionally hiss, moan or bellow. When courting female giraffes, male bull giraffes cough to attract attention.

ERROR #1

SHARKS HAVE NO ENEMIES OTHER THAN HUMANS

Few creatures seem more terrifying than a shark. Some sharks are spectacular predators, powering through the water with up to 300 razor-sharp teeth.

But sharks can also be injured or preyed upon by other animals besides humans. Killer whales, sperm whales and even dolphins will occasionally attack and kill sharks. Shark species also prey upon each other. Tiger sharks are known to have eaten nurse sharks, while smalleye hammerhead sharks are a snack for bull sharks and great hammerheads.

ERROR #2

TORTOISES ARE THE LONGEST-LIVING CREATURES

Some species of tortoise can live for 150 years or more. Jonathan, a Seychelles giant tortoise, may have been born over 185 years ago, when William IV was Britain's king and the USA were on their seventh president.

But he's not the oldest of all. The rougheye rockfish is thought to have lived for up to 205 years, while bowhead whales may live for up to 200 years. The ocean quahog clam may live up to 400 years and all these old-timers are eclipsed by black corals, found in the Gulf of Mexico, which have been dated at 2,000 years old.

IN CONTRAST, THE POOR MAYFLY ONLY LIVES FOR ABOUT A DAY AFTER IT HATCHES. IN THAT TIME, IT HAS TO FIND A MATE, REPRODUCE AND LAY EGGS, BEFORE DYING!

ERROR #3

COLONIES OF LEMMINGS LEAP OFF CLIFFS TO THEIR DEATHS

Some lemmings are believed to migrate in large numbers from place to place, but are they so silly as to fall off a cliff? Viewers of a 1958 Oscar-winning documentary, called *White Wilderness*, were made to think so as they watched lemmings leap off a cliff into what the film's narrator said was the Arctic Ocean.

The truth is different. Lemmings have never been filmed leaping to their deaths in their native habitats. The film was shot in the landlocked Canadian province of Alberta, a place where lemmings aren't found, so small numbers were imported from the Arctic Circle. Instead of *choosing* to jump, they were swept off by crew members with brooms. It was all staged for the film.

INSECT BITES

ERROR #1

THERE ARE 10 TIMES AS MANY INSECTS AS THERE ARE PEOPLE

Our planet teems with insects, far more than you might realize or can count. Their numbers are HUGE.

Here's an example – a soybean plant can support about 2,000 aphids and there may be 400,000 plants in a hectare, so that's 800 million aphids in a single field. One estimate reckons there are some 10 quintillion (10,000,000,000,000,000,000) insects on Earth. If this is divided by the human population of 7.5 billion, it gives over 1.3 billion insects per person. Mind-blowing!

SCIENTISTS HAVE SO FAR NAMED ALMOST 6,500 DIFFERENT SPECIES OF MAMMAL, BUT MORE THAN 1,000,000 SPECIES OF INSECT.

ALL MOSQUITOES BITE

Of course, some mosquitoes will leave you with an irritating spot. In parts of the world, they spread deadly diseases such as malaria. But male mosquitoes cannot bite at all. Instead, they feed on plant sap and nectar. Not all female mosquitoes bite humans either, and when they do, they don't actually bite. Instead, they pierce the skin with their long, pointed mouthpart, called a proboscis. It has two tubes. One injects saliva, which contains substances that stop blood clotting, while the other draws out a little blood.

IF IT'S FEELING PARTICULARLY HUNGRY, A MOSQUITO CAN DRINK UP TO THREE TIMES ITS WEIGHT IN BLOOD!

ERROR #3

COCKROACHES COULD SURVIVE A NUCLEAR BOMB ATTACK

Yes and no. Make no mistake – cockroaches are ridiculously tough. They can live without food for months, without air for almost an hour and can even survive for several weeks with their head chopped off! When exposed to a similar level of radiation as was given off by the atomic bombs of World War II, some cockroaches survived. These guys are hardcore.

But a nuclear weapon today would generate even higher levels of radiation. The physical force of the explosion would decimate any cockroaches close by. Though cockroaches hate the cold, they couldn't live with the extreme heat generated close to a nuclear weapon blast. Temperatures could reach as high as several million degrees Celsius. Simply scorching!

CANINE CONFLICTS

ERROR #1

DOGS SWEAT BY PANTING

As long as 14,000 years ago, dogs may have been the first species to be domesticated by humans.

Dogs have since become popular pets, but do you know all the facts about your pooch? A dog's skin doesn't contain sweat glands and dogs sweat only a tiny amount through the pads on their paws. They mostly cool off by panting. This is when a dog lets its tongue hang out of its open mouth and takes lots of breaths in through its nose and out through its mouth. As a result, moisture from its lungs and mouth evaporates, and this helps the dog to cool down.

ERROR #2

CHOCOLATE DOESN'T HARM DOGS

Yes it can. Chocolate is made from cocoa beans, which contain a substance called theobromine. A large dose of theobromine can cause pooches to vomit, suffer seizures and even die. Choc drops for dogs are low in theobromine, but most chocolate made for humans can be extremely harmful to dogs.

A DOG'S NOSE HAS 400 MILLION SMELL RECEPTORS, WHILE HUMANS ONLY HAVE ABOUT 6 MILLION.

ERROR #3

A DOG IS SICK WHEN ITS NOSE IS DRY

Most dogs' noses are cold and slightly wet to the touch because some of their tear glands empty onto their nose. A warm or dry nose doesn't necessarily mean that a dog is poorly, nor does a cold or wet nose guarantee that a dog is in great health. Canine noses may turn wetter, cooler, or drier and warmer throughout the day.

ERROR #4

A WAGGING TAIL MEANS A DOG IS HAPPY

Not always. But many postal workers have been fooled into thinking this! A wagging tail can mean many things, from excitement at seeing their owner (or dinner) to fear when faced with a threat. Italian neuroscientists and vets found that dogs tended to wag their tails more to the right when happy, and more to the left when feeling hostile or under threat.

MANY ANCIENT ROMAN MOSAICS FOUND AT POMPEII AND ELSEWHERE WARNED VISITORS TO CAVE CANEM, MEANING 'BEWARE OF THE DOG'.

HABITAT HOWLERS

A SINGLE CAMEL CALLED HARRY WAS SHIPPED FROM THE CANARY ISLANDS, OFF THE NORTHWEST COAST OF AFRICA, TO AUSTRALIA IN 1840.

ERROR #1

MOST WILD CAMELS LIVE IN AFRICA

Camels are called the 'ships of the desert', so you'd expect lots to live wild in the Sahara desert. But you're not even close...

Nearly all camels in Africa are domesticated and used by humans for transportation, as well as for their milk and meat. Small herds of wild camels are found in the Gobi desert in China and Mongolia, but only about 1,000 in total. In contrast, there are at least one million camels roaming wild in the Australian outback. Camels were first introduced into Australia in the 1860s. More than 10,000 camels were brought over to help explore and transport supplies, until they were replaced by motor vehicles. Released into the wild, Aussie camels have multiplied. That's a whole lot of humps!

ERROR #2

MOST TIGERS ARE FOUND IN INDIA

These beautiful big cats were once found throughout Asia, from Turkey and Russia through to India, Nepal, Southeast Asia and China. Their numbers have been slashed due to hunting and habitat destruction. There are estimated to be as few as 3,800 tigers left in the wild. India is home to the largest wild tiger population with about 2,900, but more than 5,000 tigers are actually kept in the USA as pets.

THE GENTOO IS THE FASTEST SWIMMING PENGUIN, ABLE TO REACH SPEEDS OF 35KM/H UNDERWATER.

ERROR #3

PENGUINS LIVE ONLY IN ICE-COLD CLIMATES

You'll never see a penguin fleeing a polar bear as they live at opposite ends of the world. Penguins are mostly found around the Antarctic Circle. Some species of penguins, though, live along the warmer coasts of Chile, Australia and New Zealand. About 140,000 penguins live along the African coastlines. Meanwhile, 970km west of Ecuador, live the Galápagos penguins, in warm temperatures of 21–26°C.

EGGSREMELY FOOLISH

ERROR #1

ALL FISH LAY EGGS

Some fish not only lay eggs, they lay loads of them. A female Atlantic cod may lay as many as 4-6 million eggs at once!

Yet, not all species of fish lay eggs. Some create eggs that develop inside the mother's body and are born as live baby fish. Many marine species, including the fearsome great white shark, give birth this way. Some sharks, such as the shortfin mako, hatch while still inside their mother, and eat other eggs before they hatch. These are called intra-uterine cannibals!

Platypus

Shark

Guppy

A STURGEON FISH MAY LAY FEWER EGGS THAN A SUNFISH OR COD, BUT THE EGGS ARE HIGHLY PRIZED – THEY ARE TURNED INTO THE LUXURY FOOD, CAVIAR.

ERROR #2

A BABY BIRD OR BIRD EGG HANDLED BY A HUMAN WILL BE REJECTED BY ITS MOTHER

Was this false fact started by parents to make kids leave young birds alone? No one knows. Apart from scavengers, such as vultures, most birds have a limited sense of smell and may not detect a human's scent. However, eggs and baby birds should be left alone. Young birds on the ground may be learning to fly. Many bird species are under threat, so collecting their eggs is illegal in a lot of countries.

Echidna

Bird's egg

ERROR #3

ALL MAMMALS GIVE BIRTH TO LIVE YOUNG

Just as not all fish lay eggs, not every mammal gives birth to live young. The monotremes, including the duck-billed platypus and echidnas, are five species of mammal that lay eggs. It take 28 days for leathery-shelled eggs to form in the mother platypus, and another 10 days to them to hatch into tiny, hairless babies. In an echidna, usually only one egg is produced, which the mother rolls into a pouch in her body. The egg takes about 10 days to hatch.

SEEDS OF DOUBT

ERROR #1

PEANUTS ARE NUTS

Some foods are not quite what you think they are. Did you know that many ice creams contain a seaweed extract? But are peanuts suffering an identity crisis?

Nuts are defined as fruits in a hard shell, which grow above ground, such as the chestnut or hazel. Peanuts, in contrast, grow underground, which means they are 'legumes' – a family of plants that includes peas. A peanut plant flowers above ground and then the stalk starts to grow down into the soil. Later, it develops pods underground containing the plant's seed – the peanut. About 540 peanuts are used to make a typical jar of peanut butter!

ERROR #2

TOMATOES ARE VEGETABLES

Tomatoes are eaten as a savoury dish. So, surely they are vegetables? Afraid not. While used like a vegetable, science knows they are a fruit. More specifically, a berry.

Tomatoes, like other fruits classified as berries, contain the seeds of a plant. Producing edible fruits is a common way for plants to disperse their seeds: the fruits are eaten and passed through the digestive systems of animals. But tomatoes are not the only fruit mistaken for vegetables – scientifically speaking, cucumbers, squash and pumpkins are also fruits.

THOUGH NOT VITAMIN C CHAMPIONS, ORANGES CONTAIN A LOT OF OTHER GOOD THINGS, INCLUDING THIAMINE (VITAMIN B1), POTASSIUM AND FIBRE – ALL ESSENTIAL FOR HEALTH.

ERROR #3

ORANGES ARE THE BEST SOURCE OF VITAMIN C

A typical orange contains about 70 milligrams (mg) of vitamin C. This equals approximately 53mg of vitamin C per 100 grams of the fruit. While this is higher than the vitamin C in mangoes (28mg), it is lower than that in kiwi fruit (93mg per 100g) and blackcurrants win hands down with 200mg of vitamin C per 100g. What's more, vegetables such as Brussels sprouts also have a higher vitamin C content than oranges with 90mg per 100g.

LEAFY LIES

ERROR #1

ALL PLANTS PRODUCE ENERGY THROUGH PHOTOSYNTHESIS

We're told that plants contain chlorophyll (found in plant cells) that enables them to convert carbon dioxide, water and light energy from the Sun into plant food, through photosynthesis.

This is all very well, but there are a number of plants that don't have any chlorophyll. About 400 species of flowering plant, including certain species of orchids, are 'myco-heterotrophs'. These plants get their food not from photosynthesis but from growing as parasites and obtaining their nutrients from fungi. Other plants, such as mistletoe, rely on becoming 'partial parasites' – growing on other plants and taking food and nutrients from them.

ERROR #2

MOSS GROWS ONLY ON THE NORTH-FACING SIDES OF TREES

Survival experts suggest this idea as a great way to navigate if you've lost your compass or GPS receiver. Factually, however, it is THEY who have really lost their way.

The claim is based on the idea that mosses prefer to be out of direct sunlight and often grow on the north-facing side of tree trunks, which are most often out of the Sun. But this doesn't work south of the Equator, where north-facing surfaces receive the most sunlight. Even in Earth's northern hemisphere, mosses can be found growing on all sides of a tree – especially if the forest receives a lot of rainfall or is very dense.

THERE ARE MORE THAN 12,000 SPECIES OF MOSS THAT HAVE SO FAR BEEN DISCOVERED AROUND THE WORLD.

ERROR #3

TULIPS COME FROM THE NETHERLANDS

The Netherlands are the centre of the tulip industry, producing about 3 billion (3,000,000,000) bulbs every year. But botanists believe that tulips originated in central Asia as a wild flower and now grow in parts of northern Africa and as far east as China. They were possibly first cultivated by the Turkish Ottoman empire, centuries before they reached western Europe from the middle of the 16th century onwards.

THE NETHERLANDS

EUROPE

IN THE 1600S, 'TULIPMANIA' STRUCK THE NETHERLANDS WITH PRICES SOARING. IT IS CLAIMED THAT PEOPLE EXCHANGED HORSES AND EVEN THEIR HOMES FOR A SINGLE BULB.

JURASSIC LARK

MAMMALS EVOLVED AFTER THE DINOSAURS DIED OUT

You wouldn't want to be a small, furry mammal during the dinosaur age, but mammals did exist.

Fossils of the mammal *Fruitafossor*, for example, have been found in North America, dating from the late Jurassic era (about 150 million years ago). Mammals in the dinosaur period were mostly small and fed on plants, insects and lizards. Many could scurry up trees if danger loomed.

THE EARLIEST KNOWN MAMMALS WERE TINY SHREW-LIKE CREATURES CALLED MORGANUCODONTIDS THAT LIVED ABOUT 210 MILLION YEARS AGO.

Fruitafossor

Crusafontia

ERROR #2

VELOCIRAPTOR WERE LARGE DINOSAURS FROM CENTRAL AMERICA

In the *Jurassic Park* films, large *Velociraptor* stole the show by terrifying and attacking humans. Real-life raptors living about 75 million years ago were not the size of a grizzly bear, as the film suggests. In truth, they were the size of a well-fed turkey: they stood less than a metre tall. The first real Velociraptor fossil was found in 1923 in Mongolia's Gobi desert. More skeletons have since been recovered, all from Mongolia, China and Central Asia. This is a long way from Central America. Like turkeys, raptors were covered in feathers.

Turkey

VELOCIRAPTOR WAS COVERED WITH FEATHERS AND HAD WING-LIKE ARMS – BUT IT COULDN'T FLY.

Velociraptor

Tyrannosaurus rex

T-REX HAD MORE THAN 50 TEETH IN ITS GIANT SKULL, WHICH MEASURED 1.5M FROM FRONT TO BACK. ITS POWERFUL JAWS COULD CRUSH BONE.

ERROR #3

THE JURASSIC ERA'S MOST DEADLY DINOSAUR WAS THE T-REX

The Jurassic era was a period of geological time starting about 201 million years ago and lasting for approximately 45 million years. Many dinosaurs lived during this time, but *Tyrannosaurus* wasn't one of them. More than 75 million years passed after the end of the Jurassic period before *T-rex* arrived on the scene. What a latecomer! While we're talking about *T-rex*, you should know that it wasn't the largest carnivorous dinosaur either. *Spinosaurus*, a monster dinosaur living in north Africa between 112 and 97 million years ago, is believed to be even larger.

SPACE DISGRACE

ERROR #1

NO EARTH CREATURE CAN SURVIVE IN SPACE

Space is a seriously hostile place. Without Earth's atmosphere, you'd be facing lethal temperature extremes and bursts of powerful radiation from the Sun. Surely, survival for any length of time would be simply impossible. Well, you'd think so...

One unusual little creature has lived in space, unprotected, and survived. A tardigrade, also known as a water bear, is a tiny creature – between 0.1 and 1.5mm long – with a barrel-shaped body and eight stubby legs. On Earth, tardigrades live mostly in water or wet mosses, but can also survive when thrown into really extreme environments.

It doesn't get much more extreme than the time when more than 3,000 tardigrades were launched on board a *Foton-M3* spacecraft in 2007. Their mission was called TARDIS (TARDigrades In Space) and it exposed them to the deadly conditions of space for 12 days. Amazingly, many water bears survived, and some were even able to lay eggs as normal.

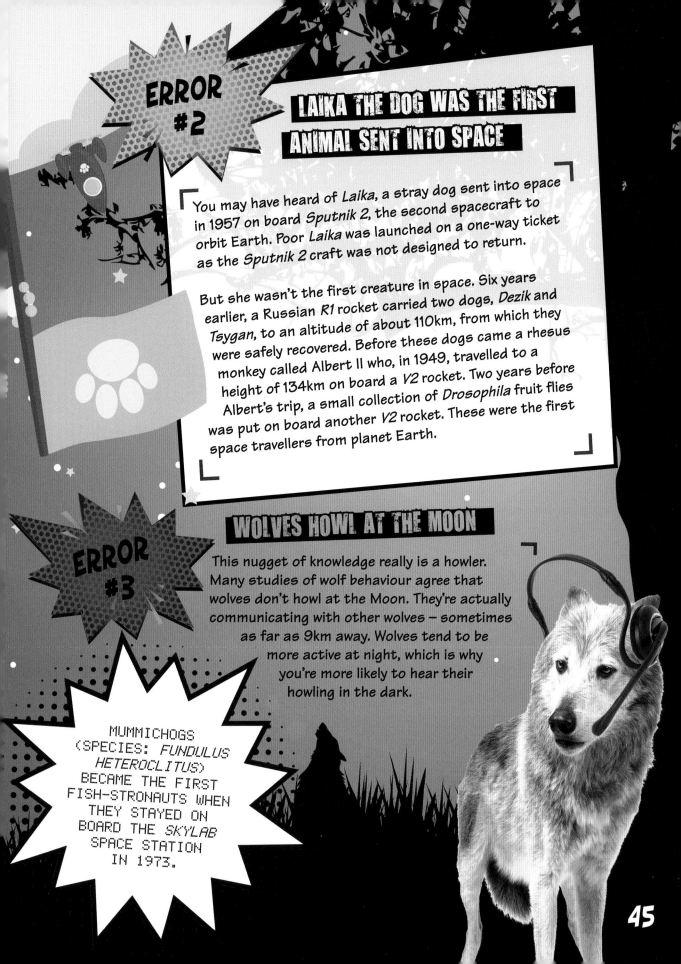

ERROR #2

LAIKA THE DOG WAS THE FIRST ANIMAL SENT INTO SPACE

You may have heard of *Laika*, a stray dog sent into space in 1957 on board *Sputnik 2*, the second spacecraft to orbit Earth. Poor *Laika* was launched on a one-way ticket as the *Sputnik 2* craft was not designed to return.

But she wasn't the first creature in space. Six years earlier, a Russian *R1* rocket carried two dogs, *Dezik* and *Tsygan*, to an altitude of about 110km, from which they were safely recovered. Before these dogs came a rhesus monkey called Albert II who, in 1949, travelled to a height of 134km on board a *V2* rocket. Two years before Albert's trip, a small collection of *Drosophila* fruit flies was put on board another *V2* rocket. These were the first space travellers from planet Earth.

ERROR #3

WOLVES HOWL AT THE MOON

This nugget of knowledge really is a howler. Many studies of wolf behaviour agree that wolves don't howl at the Moon. They're actually communicating with other wolves – sometimes as far as 9km away. Wolves tend to be more active at night, which is why you're more likely to hear their howling in the dark.

MUMMICHOGS (SPECIES: *FUNDULUS HETEROCLITUS*) BECAME THE FIRST FISH-STRONAUTS WHEN THEY STAYED ON BOARD THE *SKYLAB* SPACE STATION IN 1973.

45

A LARGE AND VERY HUNGRY ANTEATER CAN GOBBLE UP MORE THAN 20,000 ANTS OR TERMITES IN A SINGLE DAY.

GIRAFFES HAVE THE SAME NUMBER OF NECK BONES AS HUMANS. IT'S JUST THAT EACH OF THESE VERTEBRAE ARE MUCH, MUCH LONGER THAN OURS.

WHEN THE DOMINANT FEMALE IN A GROUP OF ANEMONE FISH (ALSO KNOWN AS CLOWNFISH) DIES, ONE OF THE LARGEST MALE FISH TURNS FEMALE AND WILL EVENTUALLY SPAWN EGGS THAT HATCH INTO NEW FISH.

CAMELS HAVE THREE PAIRS OF EYELIDS. THE FIRST TWO PAIRS (UPPER AND LOWER EYELIDS) KEEP DUST OUT OF THE EYES. THE THIRD IS A PAIR OF THIN MEMBRANES THAT CAN BE SEEN THROUGH DURING A SANDSTORM.

ACCORDING TO THE NATURAL HISTORY MUSEUM IN LONDON, ENGLAND, 80 PER CENT OF THE CALORIES CONSUMED BY THE WORLD'S HUMAN POPULATION COMES FROM JUST SIX TYPES OF PLANTS: RICE, WHEAT, MAIZE (CORN), POTATOES, SWEET POTATOES AND CASSAVA.

SNAKES CANNOT SLINK BACKWARD. THEY CAN PERFORM QUICK, SHARP U-TURNS TO CHANGE DIRECTION, BUT THEY CANNOT SLITHER IN REVERSE.

A LARGE OAK TREE CAN ABSORB ENOUGH WATER FROM THE GROUND IN A SINGLE DAY TO FILL SEVEN BATHTUBS.

SURF!

www.nationalgeographic.com
The official website of the National Geographic Society is packed full of information about habitats and living things.

www.nhm.ac.uk/dino-directory.html
Search for reliable facts and details about more than 300 dinosaurs at the Dino Directory, based at the Natural History Museum, London, UK.

www.goodzoos.com
A great resource, listing dozens of zoos and wildlife centres you can visit, searchable by country.

READ!

Kingfisher Animal Encyclopedia – by David Burnie (Kingfisher, 2018)
Detailed encyclopedia covering every animal out there to brush up on your animal kingdom knowledge.

VISIT!

Gawp at the stunning array of creatures and features at this museum, which includes a cutaway camel and a full-size blue whale.
The Natural History Museum, Cromwell Road, London SW7 5BD, UK
www.nhm.ac.uk

Gaze at the world's largest indoor rainforest and investigate hundreds of different plants growing at this amazing visitor attraction.
The Eden Project, Bodelva, Cornwall PL24 2SG, UK
www.edenproject.com

See some of the world's most endangered species, including rare bats, lowland gorillas and lemurs at the zoological park set up by author and naturalist, Gerald Durrell. Durrell Wildlife Park, La Profonde Rue, Trinity, JE3 5BP, Jersey
www.durrell.org/Wildlife/visit

TRUTH TREK

INDEX